HOW TO CONTROL YOUR ANGER: Perfect Guide To Manage Your Anger

Steve Jury

Table of Content

Chapter 1

What is Anger

Anger is a trademark, but sometimes unfortunate or counter-intuitive, feeling that everybody experiences once in a while. Anger experts portray the inclination as a fundamental, ordinary inclination that has been created as a way to deal with squeezing by and safeguarding yourself in light of what is seen as wrong-doing. Delicate disdain may be invited on by feeling depleted, engaged, or exasperated, in actuality, we will undoubtedly feel upset if our fundamental human prerequisites (food, cover, sex, rest, etc) are not met or are jeopardized to a great extent. We could end up being incensed while answering disappointment, investigation, or danger and this isn't exactly a horrendous or inappropriate reaction. We can in like manner feel irritated by others' convictions, evaluations,and exercises, and subsequently, shock can impact our ability to confer really - making us bound to say or do ridiculous or senseless things.

Being unbelievable or counter-intuitive can lead others around us to feel split the difference, irate or incensed themselves and, again, these can all be limits to reasonable correspondence. Anger can in like manner be a 'discretionary inclination' to feeling hopeless, frightened, subverted, or forsaken. It is significant to endeavor to get a handle on the justification for why you (or someone else) is feeling incensed at some irregular time so the fundamental drivers can be tended to and issues handled. Anger, in any case, isn't just a point of view. Anger can set off real changes including an extended heartbeat, circulatory strain, and levels of synthetic substances, for instance, adrenaline setting us up truly for 'endurance'. As a result of these genuine effects, long stretch shock can be obstructing prosperity and flourishing.

Anger can be conveyed in various ways; different kinds of shock impact people differently and can seem to make changed exercises and signs of shock. The most notable signs of shock are both verbal and non-verbal. It might be apparent that somebody is perturbed by what they say or how they say it, or their way of talking. Anger can in like manner be imparted through non-verbal correspondence and other non-verbal signs: endeavoring to look genuinely more noteworthy (and along these lines truly frightening), looking, scowling, and grasping of grip hands. Certain people are genuinely proficient at consolidating their disappointment and seeing any real signs may be inconvenient. It is, nevertheless, peculiar for a genuinely real attack to occur without 'early notification' signs appearing first.

At a principal, instinctual level disdain may be used as a technique for protecting a region or family members, securing or shielding mating respects, defending against loss of food or various possessions, or as a response to other saw dangers. Various reasons can be very different - every so often practical and from time to time preposterous. Counter-intuitive shock could suggest that you object to administering Anger or regardless, enduring that you are incensed - our page on Anger Management covers ways that you can understand and manage your disdain (or that of others).

A couple of ordinary triggers of Anger include: Trouble or possibly inconvenience, loss of a family member,or another treasured one. Discourteousness, poor social capacities,or possibly lamentable assistance.

Drowsiness, since people could have more restricted tempers and be more acrimonious when tired.Disgracefulness:for example double-crossing, being badgering, humiliated or embarrassed, or being educated that you, or a companion or relative, has a troublesome infection.

Sexual dissatisfaction Cash issues and the tension related to commitment. A couple of kinds of tension, preposterous deadlines, and things past our close control, for instance, being abandoned in busy time gridlock.

STAGES OF ANGER

Annoyed: Studies have shown that a great many people become annoyed a couple of times each day, and this is an indication that a person or thing is marginally troublesome or disturbing to you. For instance, somebody might have involved the last spoon in the lunchroom at work without recharging the stockpile. This leaves you feeling somewhat annoyed. At this degree of outrage, it's really smart to survey any contemplations that are going through your head. Since your adrenaline levels are still generally moderate, you'll have the option to contemplate a portion of the explanations for your inconvenience judiciously. You'll likewise have the option to decide whether your indignation is legitimate, and you'll have the piece of the psyche to track down a sensible arrangement. Taking the case of the spoon, investigating your contemplations can assist you with deciding whether your inconvenience comes from your disturbance at collaborators who seldom supplant things, or on the other hand if maybe this was a disconnected occurrence and your restlessness is because of simply being excessively ravenous. In light of what you conclude in the wake of checking on your viewpoints, your answer may be to either pass on a note for your collaborators to be more circumspect or essentially 'let it proceed to have your lunch all things being equal. Similarly, as with all phases of outrage, the trigger for your inconvenience can either be your interior contemplations or an outside occasion. During seasons of moderate displeasure thinking carefully is the most effective way to decide this and track down a sensible arrangement

Frustrated: At the point when outrage heightens past a less than overwhelming irritation and you feel your feelings of anxiety start to rise, you've moved into the condition of dissatisfaction. Here, you'll in any case ready to think carefully to think objectively, but since of your elevated feelings of disdain or disappointment with what's going on, it probably won't be as simple to remain mentally collected and perceptive. That is the reason it's great to acquire some actual unwinding strategies as of now, like quieting breathing, muscle unwinding procedures, and alleviating certifications

Hostile: Antagonism will in general happen when there has been an enormous development of stress, torment, or nervousness in your life. Your capacity to bear disappointing occasions is excessively low for you to have the option to adapt to tranquility any longer. This can happen for various reasons, for example, encountering an excess of physical or close-to-home agony, being over-burden with liabilities, going through hormonal irregular characteristics, or not understanding how to communicate your feelings in manners that guarantee they won't stall 'out' within you. Aggression is the stage where your outrage will in a general bubble up and out of you before an answer can be found to assist with lightening it. Right now, the body's 'survival' situation that is set up to caution you of peril dominates. Since this reaction influences the cerebrum by hosting the parts answerable for directing social way of behaving and appropriate preparation, attempting to 'think' your direction down from your aggression will most likely just outcome in additional dissatisfaction and outrage. Regardless of whether you've become effectively hostile with someone else and are snapping or hollering, there are still exceptionally compelling ways that you can settle yourself back into a more tranquil and loosened-up state to turn what is happening near.

Enraged: This is the stage when you feel all the way crazy. You might display a disastrous way of behaving when your indignation arrives at this point, such as becoming suddenly angry genuinely, over-the-top swearing, or compromising viciousness. This happens rapidly, before the levelheaded focal point the has opportunity and willpower to intentionally contemplate your displeasure, and the endurance community dominates. You could wind up enraged for the overwhelming majority of the very reasons that started your aggression, and arriving at this stage may likewise demonstrate that your 'responsive' cerebrum focus is for the most part more dynamic than your 'arranging' mind focus.

UNDERSTANDING TYPES OF ANGER

Self-assured Anger
Self-assured anger is viewed as a productive type of anger articulation. As opposed to keeping away from a discussion or being inclined to explosions of shouting or hollering, self-assured anger is utilized as a solid

and useful articulation of dissatisfaction to roll out a certain improvement. Self-assured anger can look like communicating how you feel in a great, safe way. For instance, you could begin an assertion with, "I feel furious when... " or, "I think... ". Self-assured anger is joined with suitable non-verbal communication and, some of the time, pre-set assumptions regarding techniques to determine or handle what is happening. This allows you the opportunity to communicate your anger in a manner that empowers positive change.

Behavioral Anger
Behavioral anger is an actual response, normal in men with anger issues. This can be dangerous as it very well might be communicated through viciousness, possibly slipping into horrendous or dislodged anger.

Behavioral anger is incautious and capricious, some of the time finishing with unfortunate legitimate or relational outcomes. Behavioral anger can present as scary ways of behaving (e.g., cornering somebody or raising your voice), tossing or pushing things, breaking things, or going after somebody. It's essential to distinguish whether your anger is slipping into this area because of potential legitimate or relational consequences.

Persistent Anger

Persistent anger is ordinarily coordinated towards others, circumstances, and even yourself, which can influence confidence. Some of the time, it can remain unnoticed while at the same time causing a great deal of harm. Persistent anger seems to be a consistent, low-level sensation of anger, disdain, peevishness, and dissatisfaction. As referenced above, it can apply to other people, explicit circumstances, or yourself. As a result of how you experience anger, you might experience issues handling and communicating your requirements, which can influence your wellbeing, feelings of anxiety, and relationships.

Destructive Anger

Destructive anger is a fundamentally undesirable encounter of anger that can have numerous adverse consequences. While there is a restricted exploration of this sort of anger, it's not unexpectedly found regarding the outrageous finish of conduct anger. This might incorporate outrageous touchiness or even scorn of others, in any event, when it isn't justified. Destructive anger can seem to be verbal or actual activities used to hurt others (e.g., tossing and breaking something critical to the individual you're furious with). In connections, this can now and again present as stalling (i.e., closing out your life partner inwardly). Destructive anger can affect numerous aspects of your life in very bad ways, possibly annihilating significant social connections.

Critical Anger
Critical anger is much of the time a response to some apparent slight, another person's imperfections (on the off chance that you feel they influence you), or a shamefulness against you or another person. Critical anger is distinguished in individuals' center convictions (a fundamental point of view or comprehension of the world); this center conviction is for the most part one of feeling like you're preferable or more regrettable over others, driving you to pass judgment

on them and become upset about their activities or articulations. Critical anger fundamentally seems to be something individuals call "legitimized fierceness," when you or another person is furious because of an apparent shamefulness or slight. This sort of anger can likewise seem to be putting others down or yelling about an apparent shamefulness. This can have pessimistic effects on your relational collaborations and may restrict your capacity to keep an emotionally supportive network. Furthermore, you might encounter sensations of forlornness and low confidence.

Overwhelmed Anger
Overwhelmed anger is capricious and can influence your psychological well-being over the long run. This sort of anger develops, particularly when

you don't track down ways of communicating or conveying how you feel. It might show itself when things hit an "edge of boiling over," or your capacity to adapt to anger and stress has been overwhelmed because of specific circumstances, sentiments, or collaborations. Overwhelmed anger can seem to be an unexpected snap of peevishness and disdain following a significant length of suppression. While the declaration of overwhelmed anger appears to be unique for everybody, it will come on out of nowhere and might be gone before by a distressing occasion.

Passive-Aggressive Anger
Passive-forceful anger is an avoidant type of articulation. This sort of anger happens when you stifle how you feel and endeavor to keep away from a wide range of struggles. It very well

may be dangerous as your confidence levels are frequently affected by anger. Thusly, passive-forceful anger can impact your connections. Passive-forceful anger, which can be verbal or physical, incorporates close-to-home restraint and evasion of contention. This might present as passive-forceful remarks (e.g., "I like your outfit, although it doesn't fit you"), mockery, or a purposeful absence of reaction. Passive animosity is most normal in the verbal structure, yet it can likewise seem to shut off non-verbal communication or persistently delayed at work.

Retaliatory Anger
Retaliatory anger is a typical response and an intuitive reaction to being gone after. It tends to be impacted by a requirement for vengeance after

encountering an apparent hurt. This sort of anger is normally intentionally focused on somebody who hurt you. It very well may be impacted by a need to oversee an occasion. You might wind up pointing your anger at explicit individuals in the wake of feeling obnoxious or truly went after. Retaliatory anger might expand distress and anger levels in connections.

Self-Abusive Anger
Self-abusive anger will in general be associated with disgrace. This kind of anger is found in individuals encountering low self-regard or sensations of uselessness and sadness. Self-abusive anger is generally used to assist adapt to these sentiments, although it just drives individuals further away. Self-abusive anger can influence you inside and remotely. It

can look like incorporating gloomy sentiments and taking them out on yourself through self-hurting conduct, liquor or medication use, unfortunate and cluttered eating, or negative self-talk (e.g., "You are a failure."). On an outside level, this can seem to be suddenly erupting or going after others verbally.

Silent Anger
Silent anger is a non-verbal, interior approach to encountering anger. Although you may not verbally express it, others can peruse that you are furious. Individuals who experience silent anger will more often than not keep these sentiments inside and permit them to develop, which can prompt expanded pressure, strain, and conduct connected with overpowering anger.

Silent anger can be an interior or outside experience. Inside, this kind of anger can make development of uncommunicated dissatisfaction, anger, and disdain, causing unjustifiable pressure and low degrees of progressing strain. Remotely, it can present as shut off non-verbal communication and look and confined or insignificant discourse and tone

Chapter 2

How to recognize if I have anger issues

Ask with regards to whether they have an anger issue and they will say no, yet in case you ask concerning whether they realize an enraged individual, it's fascinating the way with regards which most will say OK. There's a lot of anger out there yet by far most battle with seeing it in themselves. One clarification may be because we expect that anger is a wild tendency given to merciless emissions. In numerous events, individuals are familiar with it when they don't control their unexpected close-to-home ejections Unfortunately, too many come to recognize their abrupt profound emissions as an unchangeable piece of what their personality is. They could feel miserable to change, in actuality. Expecting that you feel that you or a companion or relative could convey anger in unfortunate ways, contemplate the going with requests, Do you or a companion or relative:

Becoming angrier than is appropriate concerning delicate disappointment or exacerbation? Feel liability or regret over something said or done in anger? Experience social battle as a result of surprising ejections of fierceness (claims, fights, property hurt, school suspensions, etc?) Have family or possibly colleagues who express concern and propose tracking down help? Oversee persevering genuine incidental effects, for instance, hypertension,gastrointestinal, inconveniences, or disquiet? Concerning anger issues, it's fundamental to know the signs and understand how to overcome them.

This keeps you protected from a close-to-home wellbeing decline, clinical issues, and relationship issues.

In right now, the news and events around you can be overwhelming, frustrating, and disheartening. This can provoke surprising emissions of fierceness that can impact your fulfillment. Taking everything into account, how might you say whether you're having anger issues?

Perturbed Verbal Outbursts
Exactly when you have anger issues, blasts are prominent. Anger can raise as a kind of mental prosperity issue including unforeseen episodes of antagonism, impulsivity, or an inconvenient approach to acting. Expecting that you have anger issues, you're unintentionally seen breaking objects, mistreating people or animals, persistent over-the-top anger, and

having temper tantrums. This antagonistically impacts your assessments, employment, and associations. Furthermore, it could achieve authentic outcomes.

Powerful episodes are ordinarily joined by:

Fuming approach to acting Gets directed up or hyper.
Successfully gets irritated.
Running contemplations.
Shaking.
Shuddering.
A dissent of chest tortures.
Palpitation or speedy unwinding.

An individual could convey dangerous verbal and genuine emissions through reprimanding someone, slapping, pushing, warming conflicts, genuine fights, mischief to properties, and assault on animals or people. Along these lines, it's critical to sort out some way to calm down or manage your anger. If you live around Kentucky, you can banter with profound prosperity capable near you if you give these signs of anger.

Consistently Haunted By The Past Accept your memory keeps on bringing back your slips up and disillusionments from a previous time. Taking everything into account, you'll most likely feel bewildered with yourself. Persistent contempt and interminable exacerbation towards explicit circumstances and others can make you angrier. Exactly when your past tortured you, sort out some way to exculpate yourself. Contribute some energy to recognize the essential wellsprings of anger to help you with pushing ahead.

Creating Hatred Towards Yourself

Cara Delevingne is only one of the various Hollywood celebrities who experienced clinical hopelessness. She zeroed in on her fight since she was a young person. In The Edit interview, she said she felt alone or separated and thought about what was wrong with her. She kept up with that people ought to appreciate her and never spun out of control with them. Taking everything into account, she turned her anger towards herself.

Expecting you to feel disdain towards yourself, it's one of the signs you have anger issues. To overcome this issue, you want to comprehend what sets off this disturbing tendency by getting a handle on the possible source and its earnestness.

You Easily Get Disappointed With The News

While self-assuredness is a significant solid area for a to overcome fear and unfairness, unexpectedly close-to-home ejections incorporate answering really, achieving antagonism. Laying out self-talk and disposing of yourself from the source is fundamental while managing this issue.

You Easily Get Irritated
Being basic is a reaction to another person's terrible structure or inadequacy. In case you're conveniently upset visiting with someone who is causing you issues, it might be a fight to make heads or tails of your sentiments.

You will as a general rule start conflicts.
You for the most part shortcoming others.

You request that your approach to acting is authentic because people around you are unnecessarily sensitive. At this point, the psyche tries to safeguard the negative approach to acting. Burden imparting your sentiments besides becoming suddenly angry to procure some sensation of control.

You feel like you can overpower others through your powerful approach to acting.

You notice that your family members, colleagues, or laborers appear to be uncertain or proceeding with caution when you're close. You unintentionally hurt others when you explode in anger.

Shallow Breathing

For certain people, shallow breathing is a distinguishable sign that someone's perturbed. In case you start seeing you're depleted, work on breathing exercises. Anger sets off your adrenaline, which is significant for your body's endurance structure. Through breathing exercises, you get to calm your body down.

Chapter 3

How to control anger in a relationship

How couples manage anger can frequently represent the deciding moment in a relationship. Try not to make do with shouting matches and hammering entryways. Anger is a characteristic and ordinary human feeling that will in general spread the word about its presence in any relationship, regardless of whether it isn't addressed to the individual to whom it is being communicated. Tragically, anger frequently raises its head in our communications with those we love the most, including our significant others. In any case, enthusiasm in a relationship shouldn't imply that feelings like anger are communicated in wild ways. Overseeing anger and dealing with your reaction to a furious accomplice is valuable expertise that can advance closeness and development in any heartfelt connection.

Avoid The Impulse to Cut Off

Stay away from the Impulse to Cut Off At the point when an individual is battling with their life partners, some of the time they might want to hammer an entryway and give them the quiet treatment. Going quiet can quiet you down for a brief time, however, expanding your accomplice's nervousness or anger is reasonable. This doesn't mean you need to plunk down and take care of an issue without giving it much thought. Rather than rapidly zooming out of the carport or leaving, consider letting your accomplice know that you want an opportunity to quiet down so you can coordinate your reasoning. Tell them that it means quite a bit to you to figure out the distinction and look at what's a suitable measure of time for you to think and return to them.

On the off chance that your accomplice will in general give you the quiet treatment when you've failed to remember a commemoration or skipped supper with their folks, you've most likely encountered some nervousness not knowing what will occur. You can't make them converse with you, however, you can share that you're prepared to share your reasoning and work together when they're prepared. Attempting to constrain or compromise them into a speedy compromise is probably going to blow up and make them cut off significantly more.

Focus on Managing Yourself (And Not Your Partner)

At the point when somebody we love is irate with us, frequently we feel a sense of urgency to conciliate and mitigate them as fast as could be expected. However, we eventually have no control over anybody's viewpoints, ways of behaving, or feelings — we're just entrusted with dealing with our own. Being quiet is significantly more powerful than attempting to quiet another person, and individuals who can remain fixed on dealing with their nervousness and responses give the other individual the space to do likewise. So rather than saying, "If it's not too much trouble, quiet down!", have a go at taking a couple of full breaths and easing back your pulse.

Essentially, if you're furious with your partner and believe they should change their way of behaving, your effort to control them is probably going to deliver a negative response. The objective is to impart your reasoning to the expectation that you'll be heard, not to disgrace the other individual. Keep in mind, that it's far-fetched that you will be heard assuming your words and ways of behaving are illuminating the apprehension reaction in your partner's cerebrum. Youthfulness brings forth adolescence so frequently in connections. It could feel basic to send a discourteous message to your partner while they're working or wake them up around midnight with your complaints, however, these procedures seldom achieve more than heightening a contention.

Know About Triangles

At the point when you're enraged or irritated at a partner, it can feel soothing to gripe to a companion, your kid, or even your specialist. At the point when we utilize a third individual to deal with our fret over another, this is in many cases called a close-to-home triangle. Needing to vent is human and it is dead on. In any case, now and again this "triangle" holds us back from figuring out the issue with the first relationship and it can leave your partner feeling detached or even make them more guarded. So whenever you're annoyed with your mate, and you're enticed to get the telephone, ask yourself, "Am I requesting help or only searching for somebody to concur with me?" If it's the last option, perhaps take a stab at quieting yourself down before requesting another person to do as such. And keeping in mind that nothing bad can be said about sharing relationship struggles with your advisor, know that they must be nonpartisan and assist you with giving your all reasoning — not to concur with you that your partner is the antagonist of the story.

Look Past the Issues

As people, there are sure points that are probably going to light a furious response or a restless response that can prompt a clash. Frequently these are subjects like cash, legislative issues, religion, sex, nurturing, or family show. It's not difficult to accept that having various conclusions can deliver anger and struggle, yet more frequently it's our youthful responses to these themes as opposed to our genuine suppositions. So as opposed to getting hung up on settling struggle as fast as could be expected, and shift your concentration back to answering as maturely as you can. This doesn't mean you want to tolerate misuse or unpredictability from a partner, or even that you need to remain in a relationship. Development looks like being willing to not allow your feelings absolutely to manage everything. It seems to be inquiring, "What is my best self doing in this present circumstance?" And you're probably not going to see the best version of yourself hammering entryways or shouting at individuals you love.

Assuming you feel overpowered by how much anger in your close connection, advise yourself that you are half of the situation. If you're more settled and more developed, your relationship will be quieter and more adult. Maybe your partner will ascend to a similar degree of development, or maybe you'll understand that the relationship isn't ideal for you. One way or another, you're deciding not to allow anger to manage everything. At the point when one individual can settle on that decision for themselves, they're probably going to find a partner who can do likewise.

Move back from the circumstance.

Take a break from whatever is driving you mad. You can go to an alternate room or even take a stroll outside. On the off chance that your partner is near, request that they let you have only a couple of moments to accumulate your contemplations before both of you talk once more. At the point when you're separated from everyone else, you can chip away at quieting yourself down and pondering what you might want to say straight away.

This is an incredible method to use during contentions or huge battles. Offering yourself and your partner a second from one another lets you both accumulate your contemplations without feelings obfuscating them.

√Gather your contemplations to keep anger from dominating:

Assuming you're chatting with your partner and they inquire as to why you're not uttering a word, let them in on that contemplating you will say straightaway. Request that they give you one minute to gather your contemplations so you don't say something you lament.

√ Know about your anger advance notice signs:

On the off chance that you notice that you're blowing up, you can utilize a method for dealing with especially difficult times to quiet down or have some time off.

√ Distinguish the wellspring of your anger:

Anger frequently covers our genuine feelings. Assuming you're experiencing outrageous fury, you could be concealing misery, responsibility, disgrace, dread, hurt, or dismissal. Pause for a minute to look at why, precisely, you're feeling irate and what can be done. For example, if you're irate about your partner's ways of managing money, you could be having an apprehensive outlook on straying into the red.
Or on the other hand, assuming you're irate that your partner is late for your supper date, you could be feeling hurt or dismissed by them.

√ Anger is in many cases brought about by horrendous idea designs: You probably won't see that you're thinking with a specific goal in mind. The initial step to fighting these negative idea designs is recognizing them, so keep an eye out for:

Δ Summing up: Saying that your partner ALWAYS follows through with something, or NEVER follows through with something. ("You NEVER make a garbage run" or "You ALWAYS cut me off while I'm talking").

Δ Accusing: Your most memorable response is to externalize fault when something turns out badly. You might fault your partner for things that happen to you as opposed to assuming liability. (If you leave your telephone on transport, you fault your partner for diverting you).

∆ Mind perusing: Assuming that your partner is intentionally harming you, overlooking you, or disturbing you. (If your partner doesn't do the dishes, you expect that they are staying away from them as a method for getting back at you).

∆ Searching for the straw that broke the camel's back or tracking down issues: Actively searching for things to be irritated about or just zeroing in on bad things. Frequently, this happens to each little thing in turn, until you come to the "straw that broke the camel's back" and detonates.

√ Cooperate to determine your issues. While you're having an issue, your most memorable intuition may be to "win" the contention. Notwithstanding, you ought to attempt to work with your partner to find a goal that fulfills both of you.

Eventually, you should both feel like you've "won."

√ Undivided attention:

It will assist with settling what is going on a lot quicker. Make an effort not to remove them when they talk and ask for follow-up inquiries to show that you comprehend. You can likewise have a go at rewording your partner's words to inquire as to whether you're understanding them accurately. At the point when you both pay attention to one another, you'll both feel appreciated, and your anger will reduce.
For instance, you could say, "I hear you saying that you believe I should think about your sentiments more and not accept you need something. Yeah?"

√ Resolve struggle by imparting a goal. Attempt to keep anger and feelings out of it, and on second thought state obviously what you might want to occur from here on out. Your partner can present their feedback and give substitute goals, however, you should both work together to serenely sort out what to do straight away.

√ The spot for pardoning:

Clutching anger will hurt you both over the long haul. Assuming you've settled the circumstance and you both feel content with the result, do whatever it takes not to clutch any feelings of disdain. Pardoning doesn't need to imply that you assume liability or even that you think what happened was alright, however it implies that you're willing to let it go. At the point when contention is settled, do whatever it takes not to bring it up again in any further conflicts. A few circumstances are hard to the point that they consume a large chunk of the day to excuse. If you don't know if you can excuse your partner, it very well might be an ideal opportunity to look for a couple's directing.

Chapter 4

How uncontrolled anger can affect your relationship with people and daily life. Anger could add to the improvement of a tremendous social occasion of heartbreaking models in affiliations. Whenever permitted to go on with uncontrolled, unanticipated discharges of furiousness and undermining ways to deal with acting will generally increment. In affiliations where peaceful, open exchange is eclipsed by rage-filled words and deeds, appreciating bonds in affiliations might be covered by critical layers of contempt.

Uncontrolled anger can be fascinating for your affiliations and your flourishing. Anger can take various plans. Certain individuals feel exasperated a tremendous piece of the time or can't quit irritating an occasion that made them insane. Others become totally off the wall every once in a while, yet when they do it emerges as dangerous episodes of furiousness. Anything that shape it takes, uncontrolled anger can inimically influence certifiable thriving and critical prospering. Research displays the way that anger and resistance can manufacture individuals' possibilities making coronary affliction, and lead to extra unpleasant results in individuals who as of now have coronary sickness. Anger can in this way concise pressure-related issues including absence of rest, stomach-related issues, and cerebral tortures. Anger lets us know we want to make a move to put something right. It reinforces us and energy and instigates us to act.

Be that as it may, for explicit individuals, anger can procure out of effect and welcome on specific issues with affiliations, work, and, incredibly, the law. In a blueprint by the Mental Health Foundation, 32% of individuals said they had a dear companion or relative who experienced inconvenience controlling their anger and 28% of individuals said they stress over how irritated they once in a while feel.

Despite the way that anger issues can impact our family, work, and public activities, a significant number of people who have them don't request help. In a relative overview by the Mental Health Foundation, 58% of individuals said they didn't have even the remotest hint of where to look for help.

By and large, individuals don't see that their anger is an issue for them and others. They ought to genuinely believe about others or things to be the issue considering everything. Certain individuals have near zero commands over their anger and will generally detonate in the exhaust. Smoldering anger could incite certifiable maltreatment or mercilessness. An individual who doesn't fight the temptation to frenzy can isolate themselves from loved ones. Certain individuals who fly into exhaust have low conviction and utilize their anger as a procedure for controlling others and feeling strong.

certain individuals consider that anger is an improper or 'unpleasant' feeling and decide to cover it.
Notwithstanding, packaged anger as frequently as potential changes into restlessness. Certain individuals vent their packaged anger at blameless social events, for example, youngsters or pets. Anger is a tendency that could be trying to conflict with and takes a more grounded confirmation to make due. Anger could trick you into thinking you are making the best decision while harming individuals around you.

1.   Anger redirects your care concerning inconsequential things. It messes up your head and dispenses with your thinking considering the thing is genuinely aggravating you to minor matters.

2. Anger misleads you into thinking your activities are correct. You become dumbfounded by your issues and attempt to legitimize your anger while faulting others for affecting you.

3. Anger outfits you with an off-course impression of assurance that forcefulness is the right reaction each time you are prompted. This makes you weak.

4. Anger misleads you into feeling that is what a genuine man/lady would do in that specific circumstance. Considering reverse opinions is most certainly not a choice when anger overpowers

Stories about working with angry people

James, Customer Service

Pretty much every guest was furious. They were furious that they couldn't recollect their secret phrase, they were irate that their Mastercard was denied, they were irate that they neglected to drop the assistance and had been paying for something they hadn't utilized for a long time. I found employment elsewhere in a stewing rage consistently, because all that outrage must be handled through me. Here and there I kicked walls, some of the time I rage cried in my vehicle before driving home, now and again I composed furious stories with furious characters who did awful things to everybody around them since they could.

I managed it as valuably as possible, yet I just lived with it for a year. If it had been a dependable profession I don't think I'd have the option to perceive myself toward the end. Everybody has their limit, and a few of us are nearer to it than we even know.

[I wish individuals knew] that their outrage didn't simply evaporate when the call finished, and that a snapshot of consideration in a furious world resembles a taste of water to somebody in an unending desert. What you do matters and affects more than you know.

Katherine, Acute Care

While working in the realm of private consideration, particularly with physically forceful and vicious youth (the vast majority of which are injury survivors themselves), it is exceptionally average to have somebody direct their displeasure towards you the entire day, perhaps the entire week — perhaps the whole length of their time there.

However, as you are there to really focus on their actual requirements, as well as help them with adapting and guideline abilities, there is a troublesome equilibrium that we needed to keep. Having youth spit on me, charge me, obnoxiously misuse me, toss furniture or individual things at me — this was important for the everyday work. Indeed, day to day.

What eventually spurred me to leave was a solitary, one-week time frame.

On a Tuesday, I had a client charge me before a stairwell with the purpose of pushing me down them. Thursday, I had a client remove the metal door handle from their bureau and toss it at my head — it hit me at the foundation of my skull behind my ear. Then on the following Monday, I had a client, corner me alone and smack me over and over upside the head until another staff part tracked down us and limited her.

Each individual I've worked with in this field has their own arrangement of stories with clients like this — stories that reach from the entertaining to the dim and vicious, hazardous recollections of somebody's annoyance, dread and injury reaction spiraling crazy.

A considerable lot of us don't adapt to it very well all things considered. At the point when I understood that my collaborators and I would go out for a beverage (read: many beverages) after each terrible shift, and how that would be pretty much each night that we'd have an awful shift, I realized I was going off course. I had the option to begin going to treatment — two times per week in any case — and work through the auxiliary injury. It was common, however, for some individuals to head the other path and self-sedate with medications, liquor, and hazardous/rash way of behaving. Turnover is extremely high in this field — a common staff part in a private home endures under a year.

I like to believe I'm one of the lucky ones, who have had the option to emerge from that experience ready to recall and handle my time there and not consider it entirely terrible. I've likewise since had other bothersome positions — at call focuses, in retail — managing irate individuals, and I'm positive that my time in private prepared me to more readily manage them and handle their outrage. I have really gotten back to that equivalent gathering home dependent upon the situation at least a time or two since at first leaving — demonstrating to myself somehow or another that I was unable to be vanquished by anything that negative things might have happened to me there.

Chapter 5

HOW DIFFERENT PEOPLE REACT TO ANGER

As referenced before, anger is simply one more feeling in an extensive rundown of totally normal and normal feelings. Through this, it's all memorable's fundamental that it is OK to feel furious — we as a whole have been angry at a person or thing previously. Anger can be a programmed response to outside occasions, e.g., loss of a friend or family member, somebody back finished you, your frozen yogurt flavor is gone at the shop, or it very well may be a response to inward occasions, e.g., you review a contention from the past with a companion and become upset once more. As a rule, anger is a reaction to torment, whether that aggravation is through feeling harmed or wiped out, feeling dismissed, or feeling undermined.

There are two principal ways that people subsequently will as a general rule answer when they feel incensed. The first is to let out all of the incensed opinions so everyone around them turns out to be more familiar with them. The second is to hold the anger inside them, disguising it from direct verbalization. Both these reactions can be dangerous.
 Responses to Anger

Many individuals respond to anger in three distinct ways;
1. Articulation
2. Concealment
While responding to anger, it's vital to do as such in a manner that won't hurt

yourself or others. Communicating anger might come to fruition through hollering, accusing, or becoming forceful.

Individuals who like to stay away from struggle could decide to smother their anger. This, in any case, could rapidly turn the anger internal. While leaving your irate considerations speechless and contemplating different things might appear to be an effective method for keeping away from anger, concealment can frequently prompt hypertension, hypertension, or misery when furious considerations are passed on to brood.

In conclusion, quieting yourself notwithstanding anger implies figuring out how to abstain from turning anger internal or over-responding ostensibly. All things considered, quieting yourself tracks down a decent harmony between communicating your anger while controlling your physiological reaction, i.e., you can bring down your pulse and circulatory strain, quiet your psyche, and so forth. By figuring out how to control anger as opposed to allowing it to control you, your forceful impulses can die down for additional practical contemplations and responses.

Allowing out the anger can be exceptionally alarming for anybody around, and the actual individual, as it can feel like the anger is crazy. In any case, gulping down all the anger can be counter-useful as well, as others don't understand there is an issue. Furious individuals may likewise feel like they have zero command over the circumstance or their own life.

For what reason do our reactions contrast?

For what reason do we have these various reactions to irate sentiments?

It very well may be made sense by taking a gander at how somebody figured out how to manage anger in youth, as youngsters figure out how to act from grown-ups around them.

A few families are uninhibited about communicating anger. They see it as supportive for somebody to act furiously when they could do without a circumstance. All things considered, anger frequently comes as result! Different families find anger unsatisfactory. Maybe it simply doesn't exist in their loved ones. So when an individual finds what is going on excruciating, they may remain silent, simply rage deep down or scowl or maybe have actual side effects. Our association hit 'Growing Up' needed to determine from an example of youngsters how they manage anger issues. So we posed the inquiry: How would you respond when you are irate?

NAME: Michelle Brown

At the point when I'm furious, I used to severely respond. Then, I would battle with the individual culpable me. The idea alone of somebody driving me mad would work up the anger in me. There was a period I trained my sibling to proceed to get water; that was his doled-out obligation at home. He would not comply, and out of anger I took a belt and lashed him brutally. This transformed into a battle. My mom mediated and I felt terrible when I saw the injury my uncontrolled anger had caused my sibling. It caused me to acknowledge that controlling one's anger is so significant. At times, one can let completely go even out in the open spots, in this way carrying disgrace to one's self and family. Along these lines, it's truly significant we figure out how to control our anger.

NAME: Joyce Drake

At the point when I'm furious individuals typically know since I make it self-evident. I never neglect to let individuals know who affront me how they treated me and how awful I felt. If the individual apologizes, it's forgotten by me, however on the off chance that the individual doesn't apologize, then I expect that is the individual's way of behaving and character. By and large, I don't beat kids who are not individuals from my family since I don't have the foggiest idea of what that could cause. Yet, I don't skewer my sibling when he begins being difficult or begins driving me up the wall since I know that regardless of whether I hurt him, my folks will deal with the costs.

There was an episode in which my sibling was playing with heated water even after I advised him to stop. Accidently, the water poured on him, I beat him notwithstanding his agony since he determinedly wouldn't submit to me. I'll guide everybody to control his/her anger as anger has landed many individuals in jail. One can carry out murder acting affected by anger, and it is a capital offense all over the place. Along these lines, we should stay away from anger at all expenses.
Other Unhealthy Ways of Expressing Anger

Hostility:

Certain individuals answer anger through forceful activity — punching, kicking, breaking things, or, more regrettable, harming others. The utilization of pernicious words as a reaction to anger is likewise undesirable and frequently damaging hostility.

Analysis:

Analysis and picking apart others are other undesirable approaches to answering anger. Rather than productively tending to the main driver of an issue, an analysis will in general exacerbate things.

Mockery:

Utilizing snide comments when you're furious additionally influences others adversely. Gnawing mockery is one certain method for harming connections.
When to Seek Professional Help

A few signs you might require proficient assistance for anger the board include:

√ Anger has driven you to genuinely or loudly misuse others.
√ Your attitude causes relationship issues at work or in your own life.
√ You stay away from specific occasions, circumstances, and even individuals for dread that your attitude will gain out of influence.
√ You've disliked the law because of unfortunate anger against the board.

Permitting out the anger can be extraordinarily frightening for anyone around, and the genuine individual, as it can feel like the anger is insane. Nevertheless, swallowing down all the anger can be counter-valuable also, as others don't comprehend there is an issue. The incensed individual may in like manner feel like they have no impact on the situation or over their own life.

Why do our responses differentiate?

Why do we have these two unmistakable responses to incensed feelings? It might be gotten a handle on by looking at how someone sorted out some way to oversee anger in youth, as young people sort out some way to act from adults around them.

A couple of families are uninhibited about conveying anger. They see it as steady for someone to act incensed when they could manage without a situation. Taking everything into account, anger as often as possible stops by results! Various families find anger unacceptable. Perhaps it essentially doesn't exist in their friends and family. So when a singular finds what's going on horrifying, they might stay quiet, essentially seethe inside or glower or perhaps make genuine side impacts.

Is there a better methodology than replying?

Is there a more steady technique for overseeing incensed opinions, which isn't such a lot terrifying but instead more controlled than letting tear, but more convincing and confident than swallowing them down? Without a doubt. The way into this approach is to appreciate that anger is a discretionary tendency. This suggests that anger is persistently covering a more essential, more significant inclination.

For example, say someone neglects to recollect your birthday, you could become unhinged with them, when altogether you are feeling hurt. Then again in case, another driver takes your parking space, you could answer resentfully anyway under you feel an inclination serious solid areas for of. Sorting out some way to recognize the principal fundamental opinions can take some preparation and can feel impossible to miss all along, yet generally a similar it justifies driving forward.

The resulting stage is to endeavor to convey those opinions rather than conveying anger, for instance, "I feel pretty hurt since you didn't remember my birthday". The other individual is getting a certifiable message about what the issue is, rather than essentially experiencing a blast of fierceness. They could attempt to will undoubtedly apologize. This way to deal with recognizing and getting a handle on feelings is an unprecedented technique for extending understanding and closeness in a relationship. It is in like manner a more confident technique for overseeing issues in the workspace.

Chapter 6

How to stop holding grudges

When you let go of a grudge, you will feel a weight taken off your shoulders. Your psyche will at this point not be obfuscated by disdain, outrage, or bitterness. To quit clutching a grudge, find a sense of peace with the present circumstance, arrive at a condition of pardoning, and continue. Take a full breath, and let go of the past!

ACCEPTING THE SITUATION AS IT IS.

Practice Empathy

See what is happening according to the wrongdoer's point of view. How could they act that way? Perhaps they had a truly extreme day at work.

Perhaps you would have responded likewise if you were to imagine being in their situation.

You can rehearse sympathy by effectively paying attention to other people, opening up to other people, keeping judgment, and chipping in.

How To Show Empathy

Listen

Listening is quite possibly the best way you can exhibit compassion to others. At the point when you are rehearsing undivided attention, you are tuning in with reason. You're not playing about on your telephone, or pondering what you will make for supper this evening, you're truly taking in what the other individual is talking about.

Assuming you're standing by listening to somebody and you get occupied by pondering supper or anything that it is you need to express next in the discussion, take yourself back to the present by saying "I was simply contemplating ____(last thing you recall them saying)__ and I was contemplating whether you could rehash what you just said so I miss nothing."

Look at the speaker without flinching (don't gaze, however, attempt to keep in touch), and sit confronting the individual. Try not to allow your look to float out of control since it will look like you're not focusing and that it doesn't matter to you what this individual needs to say. (Eye-to-eye connection is socially based. Certain individuals feel it's inconsiderate and numerous mentally unbalanced individuals feel in a real sense undermined by it. On the off chance that you don't know, ask what they would like.)

Undivided attention requires three things. To begin with, rework what the individual said to show that you grasped the substance. This is general listening expertise too. Second, reflect on your close-to-home response. Reflecting your feelings is a critical piece of compassion since it helps the individual better comprehend and manage their feelings. This is a central justification for why we require sympathy from others. Their responses assist us with controlling our reactions and figuring out it on the planet. Third, show how your reaction makes you need to act. Communicating your way of behaving is another key component because again you are exhibiting that you comprehend their close-to-home state and assisting them with sorting out a way of behaving to push ahead with.

Withhold Judgement

This is a significant step while rehearsing compassion and while rehearsing care. It tends to be truly difficult to keep quick judgment, particularly while first gathering or collaborating with somebody. But, this is an essential step toward being empathetic.

[1]Attempt to acquire a more profound comprehension of another person's viewpoint without quickly saying that it is terrible or great. In this manner, you're ready to get to a more profound degree of understanding. This doesn't be guaranteed to imply that the other individual is correct or great, however, getting some margin to acquire a more

profound point of view will help you in creating sympathy towards them.

[2]It is not necessarily the case that if somebody is acting unforgivably (expressing bigot or chauvinist things or acting like a domineering jerk) that you shouldn't mediate or say something. Shouting out is a demonstration of mental fortitude and sympathy.

Making snap decisions about others is an essential part of being human. We fostered this capacity from our progenitors to peruse possibly risky individuals and circumstances. Nonetheless, this intrinsic component can be difficult to abrogate.

The following time you wind up making a snap judgment about someone else, attempt to supersede this judgment by 1) Looking further at the individual for ways you can feel for a circumstance the individual is going through. 2) Noting a couple of things this individual presumably shares practically speaking with you (when we can uncover generally shared characteristics we are less inclined to pass judgment on others). 3) Asking the individual questions, so you can get familiar with their interesting story.

Open Up

Simply paying attention to somebody won't construct an extension among you. Opening up genuinely is an unbelievably troublesome and fearless thing to do yet it will extend the association with someone else. Sympathy is a two-way road. It's tied in with sharing weaknesses and a close-to-home association. To genuinely rehearse sympathy you need

to impart your inward scene to another person as they respond
This doesn't mean you need to spill your biography to each individual that you meet. You get to conclude who you will impart yourself to, yet, to rehearse compassion, you must be available to the chance and the chance of opening up, particularly with individuals you least anticipate.

When you find a person with whom you might want to be more open, attempt the accompanying: as opposed to resting on considerations or conclusions in the discussion, endeavor to communicate your sentiments about a given subject. Attempt to begin your sentences with "I", or in the principal individual. For instance, "I'm extremely happy we got to hang out today." Finally, shun responding to an inquiry with "I don't have the foggiest idea", particularly on the off chance that it is an individual inquiry. Individuals frequently answer in this manner to keep from going further with someone else. Attempt to think of a response that communicates how you feel.

Offer Physical Affection

Presently, you can't do this for everybody and you ought to ask before you give somebody actual warmth to ensure that it's alright (regardless of whether you've known them for a little while). Showing actual friendship, nonetheless, can help oxytocin levels and cause both of you to feel better.[3] On the off chance that you realize the individual well, give them an embrace, or put an arm around their shoulders, or a hand on their arm. Not in the least does this show that your consideration is centered around them, however, it makes an association among you.

Oxytocin has been known to assist people with better interpreting others' feelings, so a consensual embrace can develop your capacity to understand individuals on a deeper level as well as the capacity to understand anyone on a deeper level the individual with whom you're identifying.

Focus Your Attention Outwards

Focus on your environmental factors and the sentiments, articulations, and activities of individuals around you. Be careful about how others you connect with may be feeling.

Notice your environmental factors, truly notice them. Focus on sounds, scents, and sights and register them deliberately. Individuals will more often than not register things unwittingly. For instance, think how frequently you've strolled or driven someplace and have no memory at all of getting from A to B. Take in your environmental elements carefully.

Research has shown that rehearsing care about your environmental factors and individuals around you makes you bound to stretch out compassion towards them and to help when somebody needs it.

Offer Help

This shows that you see what somebody is going through and you need to make life simpler for them. Offering assistance is an extraordinary demonstration of compassion, since it shows that you're willing to remove time from your day to work on something for another person without asking anything in return.[6]

Offering assistance can be pretty much as straightforward as keeping the door open for a similar individual's structure as you, or purchasing an espresso for the individual behind you in line. It very well may be essentially as large as assisting your granddad with setting up his PC and talking him through how it functions. Or on the other hand, it tends to propose to deal with your sister's children for the end of the week so she can have some time off.

Indeed, even contribution the chance to help, can be a sympathetic signal. Let a companion that know if they need anything they can ask, opening up the way for giving assistance and backing.

2.Think about times when you hurt others.

Recollect when your sibling pardoned you for calling him mean names? Consider when others have pardoned you, and stretch out comparative sympathy to the individuals who you think violated you

3. Compose your contemplations and sentiments in a diary.

Record your record of the circumstance. What occurred, for what reason would you say you were upset, and who violated you? This will assist you with perceiving that the trouble you feel is from made feel horrible you. Letting everything out onto the page assists you with figuring out your sentiments. [3]
Recording all that will discharge your psyche of any stuff related to the resentment. Getting out those contemplations will offer you more space to occupy the space with

positive considerations and assist you with giving up.

4. Share how you feel about the circumstance with a friend or family member.

Discuss your resentment and the sentiments related to a confided relative or companion. They can offer a viewpoint to consider, similar to that the time has come to converse with the individual who upset you or that the time has come to relinquish a previous separation. Offering to others will likewise assist you with seeing precisely the way that you feel.

GETTING TO THE PLACE OF FORGIVENESS

1.

Identify what needs healing. Concentrate on the real issues at hand. Consider on the off chance that the circumstance was a consequence of miscommunication or misconception. Who is to blame, and who should be pardoned? Sort out some way to address the issue and who to pardon by first comprehension the reason to start with.[5]

Contemplate the impacts the resentment has had on you.

Do you get yourself not confiding in others?

Do you wind up acting bad-tempered and furious on a more regular basis?

Is it true or not that you are encountering actual issues like stomach torments or cerebral pains?

Have you changed your schedules because of the offense?

After you think about the resentment's consequences for you, approach yourself who it is helping for you to encounter all of that.

Does it tell the guilty party anything?

Is the guilty party irritated by it?

Is it safe to say that you are hoping to "get back" at the individual in some way?

How successful is the resentment? Is it simply harming you?

2.

Recognize what occurred and how you feel. Perceive your feelings and the truth. Coming clean about your sentiments to yourself will assist you with recognizing the hurt you feel. Try not to deny the occasion, and go over the current realities of what happened. Was what was happening nothing to joke about? On the off chance that, do whatever it takes not to relinquish it.

Provided that this is true, you ought to discuss it with the guilty party.

At the point when you assess what is happening, step back and consider on the off chance that this resentment merits your opportunity to seek after or to harp on. Some of the time you can relinquish the resentment without talking about the circumstance with the guilty party.

Inquire as to whether holding the resentment is about you or them.

Stretch out sympathy to whatever caused the injury, and let it go. After you see precisely the exact thing that occurred and how you feel, track down shared characteristics with regards to why your guilty party might have acted how they did. When you understand that you got in a battle with your companion since she just lost her employment, it will be more straightforward to relinquish your bad sentiments.

3.
Recollect that pardoning is an interaction. Some of the time it takes different discussions to come to a comprehension. Indeed, even little injuries might be investigated and pardoned once more. Show restraint toward yourself and attempt to continuously think emphatically.

LETTING GO AND MOVING ON

1.If it's something you want, try to make amends with the person. Get in touch with the person who upset you. Share your feelings with them and ask them to talk about what happened. Clearly state your displeasure with their remarks or conduct.

You have two options when your offender apologizes: accept it or say you're still not over it.

You may say, "Hey Joe, remember last week when you said the blue dress I was wearing was ugly? I was genuinely hurt by that, and I've been angry ever since.

2Deal with problems as they arise to stop them from happening again. Talk to someone as soon as they do something that annoys you. If you keep your feelings of wrath and anxiety inside, it will only feed your resentment. To go forward, you must express your feelings.

Don't hold out for someone else to express regret. They might not be aware that you are angry with them, and it fosters an attitude of entitlement.

3.Accept the apologies and move on from the incident or the offender. When you forgive, you're trying to put the issue behind you and come to an understanding with the other person. This does not imply that you are endorsing their behavior; rather, it indicates that you are choosing to let the offense and its impact on you go to move on.
Giving others the benefit of the doubt encourages them to alter their conduct and avoid future disagreements.

4.Release the negative feelings brought on by the circumstance. You are repeatedly traumatized yourself every time you bring up the grudge and sentiments of bitterness. By letting go of the resentment out of love and respect for yourself—you deserve to be happy—you may avoid this.

Remind yourself that you are only in control of how you react to a certain scenario and that you have no influence over how the other person feels. To avoid feeling responsible for other people's feelings, reaffirm these boundaries in your head.

You must decide to forgive the other person to let go of your resentment, which begins with letting go of the bad feelings you associated with the incident.

After that, you'll feel lighter and happier.

5.Don't hold individuals or circumstances to expectations. If you have expectations, you are putting yourself in a position to be let down unless your desired outcome occurs. Stop expecting things from people and your life; instead, concentrate on maintaining your health and happiness.

If you do have expectations for a circumstance, be sure to communicate them to the other party so they are aware of what has to be done to meet them. Because the other person cannot read their mind, people who neglect to express what they desire to the other person are setting themselves up for disappointment.

Without expectations, you are less likely to become offended when someone doesn't live up to them, and as a result, you are less prone to harbor resentment.

6.Take emotional care and act in your own best interests. You may feel emotionally exposed or worn out after acknowledging your emotions and talking them out. Take care of yourself by having fun or getting help from a loved one. Recognizing what you require can help you respect yourself in the choices you make regarding the apology.

Break up with someone if you can't date them after they cheated on you out of respect for yourself.

Take a relaxing bath or go for a stroll in your preferred park as a lovely treat for yourself. By doing this, you'll be kind to yourself and get rid of any leftover feelings of resentment.

Chapter 7

It is time to be happy.

STRATEGIES TO KEEP ANGER AT BAY

Do you rage when somebody removes you in rush hour gridlock? Does your circulatory strain rocket when your youngster won't participate? Outrage is a typical and, surprisingly, solid inclination. However, managing it positively is significant. Uncontrolled resentment can negatively affect both your well-being and your connections. Nonetheless, you can defeat that outrage, yes. One must initially perceive that he/she has an issue like whenever you lash out you do things that you will lament later

Prepared to return your outrage to normal and be cheerful?

Begin by considering these 10 displeasure the board hacks.

1. Think before you talk:
Seemingly out of the blue, it's not difficult to say something you'll later lament. Take a couple of seconds to gather your contemplations before saying anything. Additionally permit others engaged with the circumstance to do likewise.
Yea, it saves you from regurgitating hogwash.

2. When you're quiet, express your interests
When you're thinking plainly, express your disappointment in a confident but light manner. Express your interests and needs plainly and straightforwardly, without harming others or attempting to control them, or raising your voice. The vast majority when they are irate respond diversely like we have prior said,

yelling, screaming, yelling, destroying things, and so forth.

3. Get some activity
Actual work can assist with diminishing pressure that can make you upset. On the off chance that you experience your displeasure heightening, take an energetic walk or run. Or then again invest some energy doing other agreeable proactive tasks.

4. Try not to hold resentment
Pardoning is an integral asset. If you permit outrage and other gloomy sentiments to swarm out good sentiments, you could wind up gobbled up by your harshness or feeling of bad form. Pardoning somebody who maddened you could help you both gain from the

circumstance and reinforce your relationship.

Do you have any idea about there are likewise a few circumstances that expects you to leave the spot? Like having a serious contention with your accomplice or somebody and you feel like you will detonate any second, simply leave.

Outrage intensifies over the long haul. Assuming it happens for days, long periods, you'll confront a point of view that might be melancholy. You might feel caught. You might have successive episodes of disappointment and anxiety with even minor aggravations and with those near you.

To be free, you need to invest some cognizant energy. The joy they will say is a choice, you tell that resentment "you have no control over me except for I have some control over you".

Presently let me pose an inquiry, do you like the things you do when you are furious? I bet you don't. If another person was in your shoes, how could you feel about that individual?

Concerning when you will be free, you must conclude that.

Critically, you don't need to accuse others of your eruption. You became answerable for what you do. It will work up responsibility in you and makes you need to change.

Try not to let yourself go, don't surrender to that hazardous displeasure. You alone can control it, you alone can stop it.

Stop it before it stops you.

5 Make the relationship your need: Maintaining and reinforcing the relationship, as opposed to "winning" the contention, ought to continuously be your primary goal. Be deferential of

the other individual and their perspective.

6 Identify potential arrangements: Instead of zeroing in on what drove you crazy, work on settling the main thing in need of attention. Advise yourself that anger won't fix anything and could exacerbate it.

7 Focus on the present. When you are in the intensity of belligerence, it's not difficult to begin tossing past complaints in with the general mish-mash. As opposed to shifting focus over to the past and allocating fault, center around what you can do in the present to take care of the issue.